THE
DREAM
SOURCEBOOK
JOURNAL

Also by Phyllis R. Koch-Sheras, Ph.D., and Amy Lemley:

The Dream Sourcebook:
A Guide to the Theory and Interpretation of Dreams

KEEPING A JOURNAL

THE
DREAM
SOURCEBOOK
JOURNAL

BY
PHYLLIS R. KOCH-SHERAS, PH.D.,
PETER L. SHERAS, PH.D.,
WITH AMY LEMLEY

Lowell House
Los Angeles

Contemporary Books
Chicago

Copyright © 1996 by RGA Publishing Group.
All rights reserved. No part of this work may be reproduced or transmitted in any form or by any means, electronic or mechanical, including photocopying or recording, or by any information storage or retrieval system, except as may be expressly permitted by the 1976 Copyright Act or in writing by the Publisher.

Requests for such permissions should be addressed to:
Lowell House
2029 Century Park East, Suite 3290
Los Angeles, CA 90067

Lowell House books can be purchased at special discounts when ordered in bulk for premiums and special sales. Contact Department TC at the address above.

Publisher: Jack Artenstein
Associate Publisher, Lowell House Adult: Bud Sperry
Managing Editor: Maria Magallanes

Text design: Laurie Young
Illustrations: Charlene Rendeiro

Manufactured in the United States of America
10 9 8 7 6 5 4 3 2 1

PREFACE

A dream is a uniquely personal experience, and sharing it with someone is a gift from one person to another. One of the greatest values of dream exploration is the way it enhances your close personal relationships. From the very beginning of our relationship more than twenty years ago, we have felt that "the couple that dreams together stays together." We first got to know each other when we both participated in a dream seminar during our clinical training. We were barely acquainted then, but discussing our dreams allowed us to see one another in a special and intimate way. Through dreamwork we came to understand each other more quickly and more deeply than we might have otherwise. In some ways sharing a dream was as personal and exciting as sharing a first kiss. It was new and exhilarating.

Since that seminar and the three intensive dream groups that followed within five years, dreams have played a major role at important stages of our life as a couple. Just before we moved into our first house, we got ideas about how to share the space with the help of Phyllis's dream called "Eight Tennis Balls." In talking about this dream, we came to see that the way she portrayed our "playing ball" with eight balls was a clue for how we might divide our responsibilities in the new eight-room house. Peter's dream "Left by the Bus," in which a small puppy is abandoned while everyone else goes off to school, enabled us to imagine how our son might feel about the anticipated birth of another child.

Dreaming "together" by mutually working on our dreams continues to bring emotional depth to our relationship. Our differences in gender and personality are assets in interpreting each other's nighttime lives. We have learned to appreciate our unique perspectives and can use dream images to explain how we feel or to construct a vision of our future.

We have been discussing dreams as a family ever since our children learned to talk. When our children were very young, we became closer to them through dreamwork. In fact, we found we were better able to advise and support them through dreamwork than by most other means. Our son and daughter even joined us in making presentations at a number of dream conferences when they were little, a truly fun and exciting challenge for all of us.

Dream sharing works well not just for couples and their children but also for friends and relatives. This journal can provide an opportunity for you to form a special relationship with your dreams and with those you love. We hope that you will record your dreams here and find their value in your waking life.

Pleasant dreams!
Phyllis and Peter

KEEPING A JOURNAL

WHY RECORD YOUR DREAMS?

Since the beginning of recorded time, people have been writing down their dreams. The Sumerians inscribed their dreams with sticks on clay tablets in 3000 to 4000 B.C., noting the same types of details that experts suggest to modern dreamers keeping dream journals. Archaeologists have discovered an Egyptian book on dream interpretation that is more than two thousand years old. Almost every culture has attributed some significance to the visions that occur during sleep. Drawing upon centuries of tradition, we can use the images we see in our sleep to enhance and enliven our waking lives. A dream journal provides a window to an exciting and mysterious land, crisscrossed by paths inviting us to gain insights about our deeper selves. Many people report that recording their dreams has a profound effect on their world view and on the way they act.

RECORDING YOUR DREAMS

Chronicling your dreams and exploring their meaning through dreamwork is both fun and enlightening. This book will teach you a method for organizing images and information to help you focus on your dreams and make the most of this hidden dimension of personal and spiritual life. There are many advantages to working with your dreams in this way.

IMPROVING RECALL

A daily practice of remembering dreams has many benefits. First and foremost, the more you do it, the easier it becomes. When you decide to make an effort to recall your dreams by writing them down, you will notice within a short period of time that you awaken in the morning aware of more dream images and dream stories. The goal of remembering dreams is most easily achieved merely by deciding before you go to sleep to write down your dreams in the morning. After a few weeks it is not uncommon to wake up with memories of more than one dream or dream "fragment." Over time you will find the number of entries in your dream journal increases.

RELATING DREAMS TO WAKING LIFE

A second advantage of the daily practice of writing in a dream journal is the development of a more "familiar" relationship with the content of your dreams. When you are used to regularly identifying the images and symbols in dreams, you are more likely to recognize these same things during the day. The opportunity to connect daytime and nighttime events can produce a sense of curiosity about the power of a particular dream. For example, if your boss calls you into her office it may remind you of a recent dream in which you were asking for a raise. Remembering your feelings in the dream can help you prepare for this event.

INCREASING LUCID DREAMING

Some dreamers say that writing down their dreams increases the likelihood of lucid dreaming. Lucid dreaming is the experience of knowing that you are dreaming while you are dreaming. You might find yourself saying during a dream, "Oh, I guess I am dreaming now." Dreamers report their lucid dreams are more exciting, vivid, and intensely emotional than other dreams. Often the realization that you're dreaming is so extraordinary that you wake up. But try to stay in the dream; the results may surprise you. During a lucid dream, you have the possibility of influencing your own actions in the dream, or even asking questions of some dream characters. You can also direct healing images and practice problem-solving techniques. You may experience increased access to creative insights. Many cultures consider this lucid state to be the most powerful type of dream experience.

NOTICING RECURRING THEMES

Recurring or common themes and images in dreams over a period of time are much more evident when there is a written record to which to refer. You can identify the influence of certain occasions on your dreams (for instance, you dream about your mother on Mother's Day, or about your brother on his birthday), and you can note the influence of seasons or significant events. You may notice that every spring you have dreams about babies, representing a theme of new growth, or that a current conflict with your parents produces dreams about staying out late as a teenager. Keeping track of recurring themes can help you interpret their meaning and answer important questions about your personal life. How do certain dream themes change over time and what do they reflect about you? Do major life changes produce dreams about old anxieties?

Do vacations produce more frequent dreams about being away from home as a child? Your dream journal enables you to examine recurring themes through a variety of techniques, including key words, drawings, and detailed notations about characters and setting. You can also note specific occurrences of lucid dreaming or dreaming in color. Remember that a dream theme can be related to both the *content* of a dream (the dream details themselves) and the *form* of the dream (the way the story unfolds). You may notice a pattern: for instance, at times when you long for more control in your life you have more lucid dreams, or you tend to dream in color when your waking life seems boring or dull.

INCREASING SELF-AWARENESS

Regular dreamwork can have a positive impact on your everyday feelings. Research shows that people who frequently recall their dreams are more likely to acknowledge their emotions and deal directly with conflict in their lives. Keeping a journal encourages you to remember things from the past that may have been painful or that have been forgotten. You may find that exploring difficult issues and confronting challenging situations becomes a regular experience in your dreams. You can enrich your personality by getting used to encountering these images and the feelings that accompany them. Your dreams may also provide ways of addressing these issues. Most people have the desire to push away negative feelings in waking life. They may avoid taking decisive action because they are frightened. Practice in dealing with dream material that might otherwise be outside your consciousness actually increases self-awareness and can prepare you to live a fuller life with less fear. Dreams become your "teachers" by informing you about a full range of wishes, fears, emotions, and solutions.

BROADENING PERSPECTIVES

People breathe air to live. Often, we forget that it is all around us until we are in a place where there is little air. It is only then that we experience air from a different perspective and learn to appreciate it. Dreams help us examine and appreciate our waking lives by offering entirely unique views of objects and characters that are familiar to us. Dreams may look strange or mysterious because they present things from an unusual standpoint. Whether we write down our dreams, say them, sing them, or draw them, they can enhance our natural creativity by providing new ways of perceiving old things. Images may be combined in fantastic ways (a snake with wings) or altered from the ordinary (your garden filled with teacups). The process of documenting what we recall by writing or drawing may encourage new ways of thinking. For example, a dreamer who envisions the house he grew up in as much smaller than before may realize that he is now more grown-up and has "outgrown" his childhood ways. Dreams spur us on to broaden our perspectives.

EXPLORING RELATIONSHIPS

By noting and remembering the people and relationships that come up in your dreams, you have the opportunity to pay attention to those relationships in a way that will enhance them in your waking life. In dreaming about particular people, you may gain insight into personal conflicts with them and discover how to deal with such problems more effectively. You may get in touch with some unrealized or unspoken feelings about someone, and once you become aware of them in the dream, you can tell that person. This is possible even if the person is no longer physically accessible. Through the dream world, you can complete unfinished business with departed friends or loved ones.

UNCOVERING THE UNCONSCIOUS

Dreams and dream symbols show us a side of ourselves we don't often see. Recalling dreams gives us ongoing access to our inner self in a way that expands our waking life. It is intriguing to think that there is a hidden part of us that motivates our behavior and experiences. Connecting with the unconscious links us with the deeper spiritual, and perhaps supernatural, part of ourselves. All dream symbols have meaning at various levels: the personal level of our individual uniqueness, the cultural level of people who share the same customs, and the universal level, which is shared by all humankind. It is this universality that goes beyond everyday events and accesses the dreamer's spirituality. This aspect of our dream life often includes exotic characters that symbolize universal ideas and themes representing some of the most powerful elements of our personality: wisdom, nurturance, fertility, thievery, trickery, and so on. While these characters may not appear very often in our dreams, when they do, they offer some important insights into our deeper nature and basic humanity.

HEALING

Another benefit of recording your dreams is that you can take advantage of their healing power. Just the act of putting a dream down on paper can be healing in itself. Like any form of meditation, slowing yourself down in the morning before launching into your day is a healthful practice. To ease the transition from sleep to waking life, take the time to write down a dream before hopping out of bed. This will enable you to feel more focused, energized, and relaxed as you go on with your day. Then read over your dream for clues as to what direction or actions you may want to take that day.

Recording a dream can also alert you to some physical condition that needs attention. Such was the case with the woman who dreamed of a large letter C emerging from her stomach. This alerted her to the need for more vitamin C in her diet; when she added it, she felt better.

Before you go to sleep, you can also "program" or direct your dreams to give you information on some part of you that needs healing. This is what Phyllis did after her knee reconstruction surgery to help her deal with the discomfort and difficulty in walking. She made a note in her dream journal asking for help with healing her knee. The next day she recorded a dream in which there was a dying evergreen tree. She drew a picture of the tree over a drawing of her knee and colored it with a healing green. As she did so, she thought about sending healing energy to it. Later that day she stopped limping and felt less pain in that knee. You can also program yourself to have a healing dream for another person. Write it down in the morning, share it with the person who needs help, and see what he or she gets from it. You might be surprised at the clues for healing that you discover in the dream.

ENHANCING CREATIVITY

Dreaming is a creative process. Even if you think, "I'm not a creative person," your dreaming mind is still at work every night imagining original and sometimes outlandish scenarios. Connecting with that creative energy by writing down your dreams will keep you more in touch with your imagination. Trust your ability to generate new images and ideas by making friends with your dreams. They are nighttime brainstorming sessions, free of inhibition and judgment. Dreamwork can enhance your problem-solving ability and give you professional, artistic, and personal inspiration.

HAVING FUN

Aside from all this serious dreamwork, you can also have fun playing with your dreams as you record them. Trust your dreams to reveal new ways of enjoying yourself. This can improve your dream recall and provide a richer, more varied dream life. Like taking care of plants, the more you give to your dreams, the more they give back. Keeping a dream journal is a way to give to your dreams and to have them give back so much to you. So let's begin cultivating your dream garden with this journal.

PREPARING THE DREAM SPACE

Start by telling yourself before you go to sleep that you will remember your dreams. This is perhaps the most important thing you can do to increase your dream recall. You may want to develop a dream ritual or statement that you say every night. Make it a habit, like brushing your teeth. It may take a little practice, but after a short time your dreams will be easier to remember. Create your own dream incubation or meditation ritual, or use one of those described in *The Dream Sourcebook* (see pages 114–116). You may want to write it in the front or back of your dream journal so that it is readily available to review before you go to sleep. Tibetan dreamworkers say this kind of dream preparation during your waking hours is most useful for getting value out of your dream life.

Put your *Dream Sourcebook Journal* right next to your bed, where you can see it and reach it easily when you awaken. Having it close by will remind you to think about your dreams before you get involved in anything else and forget them. Make sure you have a pen at hand so that you don't have to search for something to write with when you awaken. We suggest that you keep a colored pen or pencil or some crayons nearby for highlighting key words or drawing dream images. You might even want to have a tape recorder available for audiotaping your dream first, and then transcribing it into your journal later. Some people find this helpful for remembering more of the dream or visualizing it more clearly.

Paying attention to the environment or "dream space" you sleep in can enhance your dream recall and the productivity of your dreamwork. Take care, especially on nights when you particularly want to recall a dream, to clear your psychic and physical space and adorn your sleeping environment with special dream effects. You may want to hang a dream drawing or dream catcher near your bed (*The Dream Sourcebook,* page 150), sleep on a dream pillow stuffed with special herbal "dream blends" (*The Dream Sourcebook,* page 187), or play some dreamlike music to relax you and put you to sleep.

THE FORMAT FOR RECORDING YOUR DREAMS

You create your own dreams and have the final word on what they mean. In the same way, only you can decide what is the best way to keep a dream journal. We offer some suggestions based on what our experience tells us works best. Try the methods suggested here. Modify them to meet your own needs if you wish, but try to be consistent in using whatever modifications you introduce. The good thing about using a format is that it gives you a regular ritual that makes it easier to recall and interpret your dreams.

SETTING UP THE JOURNAL

The first thing to do in preparing to record a dream, either the previous night or when you wake up, is to write down the date and day of the week on the page (we suggest the upper left-hand corner). You may use either the date of the night you go to sleep or the date of the morning you awaken. It doesn't matter which you use as long as you do it the same way each time you record a dream. Noting the day of the week with the date may help you remember what was happening in your waking life on that day, which will provide some clues when you later interpret the dream. If you are away from home, also indicate the city you are in.

Before you go to sleep, you might also want to write down at the top of the page a problem or an issue you are dealing with in your waking life. This allows you to program your dreaming mind to give you some ideas for dealing with the issue. You could write down something like, "I will dream about how to deal with my mother-in-law's visit in an effective way, and I will recall and record it when I awaken" or "I will dream about the pain in my chest and receive clues for how to heal it that I will recall when I awaken." This kind of dream "incubation" can bring a particular answer or dream message. Don't be concerned if you do not see the connection right away; just take whatever you get and see what comes to you after using some of the other dreamwork techniques described here. If you don't remember your dream the next morning, don't be discouraged. Keep programming your dreams until you get something. It will come eventually.

R&R: RECALLING AND RECORDING YOUR DREAM

The next step is the R&R of dreamwork, that is, dream recall and recording practices. They are every bit as important to our well-being as the other kind of R&R, "rest and relaxation."

Recall your dream. Before you can record a dream, you must recall it. To maximize your chances of remembering a dream, keep your eyes closed, don't move, and don't think about what you have to do that day. Just lie still and notice any images or dream stories that come to mind. There is always something to recall, because everyone has several dreams each night. If nothing comes to you right away, try shifting to different positions in bed. This may jog your memory and bring more images to mind. Sometimes you'll remember an image from the end of a dream, and you can work backward to retrieve the whole story. Or you'll become aware of a strong feeling connected to something in your life that triggers a dream image. Let your mind wander to the previous day's feelings or to the thoughts you had just before retiring; sometimes that will trigger a dream memory or fragment. Whatever you get, run through it in your mind once or twice as though you were watching a movie. You might want to say the dream aloud or tape-record it to help crystallize it in your mind. Be open to remembering more details of the dream when you write it down. Still more may come back to you later in the day; certain events or people you encounter may trigger memories of other details and may even prompt the recollection of another dream.

Record the Dream. Now that you have some recall of your dream, reach for *The Dream Sourcebook Journal* and a pen and start writing on a new page of the journal. If you haven't done so already, write down the date and day. Then begin writing down your dream in the first person, present tense, as if it were happening right before your eyes, or as if you were telling a story. For example, "I am walking down the street in front of my house when I hear a loud noise." Make a concerted effort to use this storytelling style. It is key to making the dream images and details come to life. Soon you will find it is the only way you want to recount your dreams or listen to other people's dreams. In regard to others' dreams, you may want to have a copy of *The Dream Sourcebook Journal* for your children. If they are too young to write down their own dreams, do the recording for them. Teach them to tell you their dreams in the first person, present tense, and to give you as many details as possible.

You should record any dream or dream fragment, no matter how seemingly trivial or embarrassing, in as much detail as possible. The details may prove to be very significant when you analyze the dream later. Like an expert movie critic, look for and record all the aspects of the dream story—location, lighting, sounds, colors, directions, speed, size, age, emotions, and anything that stands out or seems different or bizarre. Make sure that you note the feelings that occur during the dream, especially those at the end. They are important clues to the dream's meaning. Note if something in the dream is different in appearance from the way it normally is in your waking life, such as the size of your house, the layout of your office, the color of your hair, the style of your car, and so on.

If you are unsure about something in your dream, write it down anyway and note your uncertainty with a question mark or by jotting down various possibilities. Ask yourself if a certain recollection was actually in the dream or just appeared as you were recording it. Write it down, note your uncertainty, and just go on. The important thing is to get it all down on paper before you lose it. You do not need to be concerned about correcting mistakes in grammar or spelling. In fact, those "mistakes" may later give clues to the meaning of the dream. Like "Freudian slips," they may be the way your unconscious mind is revealing your true feelings. In any case, don't worry about being "correct." As long as you will be able to recognize what you wrote later, it really doesn't matter. Your dream journal is for your eyes only, and it won't be graded!

Title Your Dream. After you have finished writing down the dream, go back to the top of the page and write down a title for the dream. This will help you in working on the dream and will enable you to locate it more readily at a later time. Choose a title that captures some key element of the dream—a major character ("The Rabbi"), a key object ("Eight Tennis Balls"), a significant event ("Nine Months to Live"), an intense feeling ("Worried About Dad"), a distinctive characteristic ("The Birthmark"), a particular message ("Walk on the Wild Side"), and so on. If you have a very long dream, you may want to add subtitles in the margin at places where the action or the scene changes. Where a new dream begins, you may want to turn to a fresh page and give the dream its own title.

Circle or Highlight the Key Words. Now is the time to take out your colored pen or markers to circle, or highlight the key words or phrases in your dream. These highlighted words will give you a starting point in working on your dream and analyzing its meaning. Be sure to mark such things as characters' names, places, objects, directions, sounds, feelings, action verbs, important adjectives and adverbs, and so on. You will be able to use these notations later on in your dreamwork when working on your various associations to parts of the dream.

Underline the Feelings. After circling or highlighting key words in the dream, underline particularly emotional parts of your dream as well. These might be particular phrases or even passages where strong feelings came up for you either during the dream or while writing it down. These emotions are important; they can be the door to a deeper understanding of your dream as a whole. You don't have to be afraid of them or think that you have to deal with them now; simply acknowledging your dream emotions can help greatly in understanding your dream and yourself.

WRITE DOWN THE FIVE Ws

Now that you have started disassembling your dream, you can use other dream work techniques to help interpret it. Like a journalist, concentreate on the Five Ws—who, what, where, when, why—to organize your dream material. Write your answers to the Five Ws in your dream journal after your initial entry or read your responses aloud to yourself, to a partner, or to a dream group.

WHO

Who are the characters in your dream? Are they people you know? Sometimes even an object can be a "who" in your dream—a school locker, or a rock or shrub that suddenly appears to have a life of its own, like in a cartoon. Dream characters need to be broadly defined. They are characters in your dream if you think they are, no matter how you might see such things in waking life.

In the dream, are you an active participant, taking action that advances the story, or are you a passive participant, subject to the actions of others? You might be an observer in the dream, watching the whole thing from a safe distance. Sometimes the "who" changes in the dream; people are transformed from one person to another or from one thing to another. Are you familiar with who is in the dream? Are you certain, or do you just have a general feeling about it? If you are not sure about a character, put a question mark next to the name. Are there special dream characters that you recognize from other dreams you have had? Take note of all these things when recording your dream.

WHAT

The *what* description of your dream journal is often the longest. It tells the story of the dream and puts the pieces together. When recording this part, try to remember as much detail as possible, even if you need to mark some parts with question marks.

What is going on in your dream? What actions are occurring? Sometimes it is difficult to know what is happening. You might need to say, "I am not sure what is happening but there seems to be some sort of dance going on."

What objects or colors do you notice in the dream? Do you see a red rose or a gold Cadillac? This is often a good way to determine if you are dreaming in color.

What relationships are portrayed in the dream? Is there fear, sex, intimacy? Are there parental feelings?

Are there symbols in this dream? Focus also on the feelings you have in the dream. What do you remember feeling? What are the feelings you have about the dream when you are remembering it afterward?

Is there one basic theme or are there a few basic themes in the dream? (Some examples of themes are friendship, betrayal, anxiety, confrontation, sadness, or competition.) You might have a dream about having a job interview where you feel very anxious and upset. The theme might be how you try to manage your anxiety or try not to look nervous.

Do you have bodily sensations after the dream? Are you tired or refreshed, agitated or calm?

Are you reminded of anything in your waking life or in past dreams?

WHERE

Where is your dream taking place? Is it a place you know, or is it a combination of places you recognize in your life? Are there noises or sounds coming from there? Take note of how you feel about this place. Is it different from the way it was in waking life, or, if you have been in this setting in other dreams, is it somehow different in this dream? If the place is not familiar, does it remind you of anything? It may be that the setting is timeless or unrecognizable. Note this as well.

WHEN

When is your dream happening? Can you tell? Are there clues as to the time of day, time of year, or time of your life? Remember that dreams can be about you at any time in the past, present, or future. Notice inconsistencies in time in your dream—for example, you are a child but there are objects around you from a later time in your life. Do you feel comfortable about time in the dream or are you confused by it?

WHY, AND WHY NOW?

Why are you having this dream, and why are you having it at this particular time? Is there something in your life now that you connect to this dream? What is it? What thoughts and events stand out? Do events of the last few days appear in this dream? Can you think of significant events in the past day or two that might explain why you are having this dream now? Did significant events occur around this date in some other year? If the dream is different in any way from your current waking life, how is it different? Are these differences there for a reason? It may be that your dream is a wish fulfillment or a worst fear. If this is a recurring dream, why are you having it again?

Though not necessarily long, the *why now?* part of the Five Ws is often the key element that gives you clues as to the meaning of your dream. Let yourself think of all the possible connections and see what you come up with.

SPEAK OR WRITE YOUR DREAM OUT IN "DREAM LANGUAGE"

Now that you have recorded all you can in ordinary language, enhance your understanding of the dream by translating it into "dream language." In doing this you will approach the dream as if everything in it represents some part of yourself. Since you created the entire dream from your unconscious, every element that appears in it not only represents some aspect of your waking life but also some part of you. Translate everything in the dream into some aspect of yourself by adding the phrase *part of me* to every object, adjective, person, or pronoun (except "I", "me"). You may even break words into syllables, and add the phrase *part of me* to each syllable ("the motor part of me," "cycle part of me"), potentially adding new insights to the material.

The other key characteristic of dream language is the idea that you are accountable for all the events and feelings in the dream. Add the phrase *have me* to the beginning of every sentence or major new phrase and to all the verbs. This emphasizes that you are responsible for creating your life, including the dream stories you make up. Thus, things do not really happen to you in the dream; you have them happen. For example, "I am beat up by a thief" becomes in dream language "I have me beaten up by the thief part of me."

It may feel awkward at first, but after you have recorded your dream in ordinary language, try saying it aloud or writing it down in dream language and notice what stands out for you. You may want to try playing different parts of you, giving yourself a message or warning from those parts.

For a more in-depth description of dream language, see *The Dream Sourcebook*, chapter 5.

ACTIONS TO TAKE

Once you have looked at your dream more closely with the help of the Five Ws and dream language, you may get a message about some action to take in your waking life. Be careful not to jump to any dramatic conclusions based on one dream, but let yourself be inspired. Write down at the end of your dream the action you intend to take and when you will have it completed. Leave room to comment on the outcome of your action.

MAKE A DREAM DRAWING

You may find it illuminating to add some nonverbal expression to your dream description. Sometimes it's easier to free up your feelings and express your ideas through art. This is especially true for young children who are not quite facile with language. Your drawings do not have to be elaborate or particularly "artistic"; even stick figures will do. Sketch an important object, character, or scene from your dreams. You might choose to draw a sequence of events from the dream in cartoon form. Whether or not you remember colors from the dream, you can enhance the mood, tone, or healing power of your drawing with color. Experiment and have fun with it. You might want to make a more elaborate dream drawing on a separate sheet of drawing paper and hang it by your bed.

Sample dream entry:

6/16/96— Sunday   *"Making the Train"*

> I'm <u>driving</u> to a <u>train station</u> to catch a train (to see my mother?). I <u>park</u> and go inside and pick up a <u>schedule</u>. I think I should have looked at the one earlier that I had in my <u>purse</u>. I look at that one and see a time of <u>2:35</u> marked

off in the bottom right-hand corner. I look at my watch and see it's almost 2:30. I think, "Perfect!" I tell Susie and David. Paul is parking the car (?). I start to buy the tickets from a machine and decide to just get them on the train even though it costs a bit more. I feel excited and pleased.

Who: Me, Susie, David, Paul, Mother
What: Catching a train, park car, schedule, costs more, works out perfectly, feel pleased and excited
When: A few years ago (when Mom was still alive)
Where: Switzerland? (rode many trains there on recent trip)
Why now?: Father's Day, traveling yesterday

Dream language translation:

I have me driving to a train part of me station part of me to catch a train part of me to see my mother part of me. I have me park and go to the inside part of me and pick up a schedule part of me. I have me think I should have looked at the schedule part of me earlier that I had in the purse part of me. I have me look at that schedule part of me and have me see a time part of me of the 2 part of me 35 part of me marked off in a bottom part of me right-hand part of me corner part of me. I have me look at the watch part of me and have me see that it's almost the 2 part of me 30 part of me. I have me think, "Perfect!" part of me. I have me tell the Susie part of me and the David part of me. I have the Paul part of me parking the car part of me. I have me start to get the tickets part of me from a machine part of me and have me decide to just buy them on the train part of me even though I have it cost a bit more part of me. I have me feel excited and pleased.

Action to take:

Talk to sister on Father's Day; share feelings about loss of Mom and Dad; take time to inquire about mother part of self; complete letters to new friends from Europe trip by June 30th.

Dream Drawing:

ADDITIONAL USES FOR YOUR JOURNAL ENTRIES

There are many other ways to use your dream journal after you have begun to record your dreams. You will begin to find your own favorite uses for your dreams and a special place on your shelf for your completed journals. Below are just a few more suggestions.

YOUR PERSONAL DREAM INDEX

At the back of this dream journal is a Personal Dream Index, where you can enter themes, key words and phrases, and symbols from your dreams. Note them alphabetically, followed by the page on which the dream appears. Each time that particular element recurs in a dream, add the subsequent page numbers. In this way, you can develop your own personal glossary of recurring dream symbols and begin to develop a sense of what is important to look at. For example, what dream images or "dream helpers" are prevalent in your dream world? If a wise old woman appears in various forms in several dreams, giving you suggestions, messages, and assistance, you might begin to see her as a character. This kind of character often recurs in dreams to assist you, lending support as you move in new directions. You can then use these figures in both your waking life and dream life to enrich and heal aspects of yourself. Keep adding to your dream index each time you record a dream. Note the key words or phrases that you have underlined, circled, or highlighted, and transfer them to the Dream Index. If you don't have enough time when recording your dream, take time to index them later. You can then go back and examine the recurrent themes and symbols that are clues to the meaning of your dreams.

ENHANCE YOUR PERSONAL RELATIONSHIPS

Dreams can tell you a great deal about your relationships: the ones you have and the ones you want to have. Note in your journal the relationships between dream characters and even the relationships between characters and symbols or objects. Do you dream a lot about relationships, or very little? In dreams you might fantasize about relationships you want but are afraid to have in waking life. Sometimes a different kind of relationship exists in a dream, more loving or more distant than the actual relationship that inspired the dream.

Partners/friends. Dreams can open up new awareness about our feelings for those we love. If you have a close friend or partner, compare journals and work on your dreams together. Use the material in the journal to share feelings, hopes, and fears. Notice how you are alike in the way you dream and in the themes and key words you have recorded. You may be surprised to find how many similarities you have with people close to you. This is a way to learn about each other. You may even have an experience of "co-dreaming": sharing a dream in the same night, dreaming about each other, or programming a dream together.

Family members. Discussing and sharing dreams with your children has many advantages. Help them keep dream journals of their own. This will teach them not to fear their dreams, and they will look to them for insight into themselves. They can "make friends" with the characters and images in their dreams and render them less frightening. Sharing your dream with your children lets them know they have a special place in your dream life as well as in your waking life. Talking about their dreams shows them you too can be excited about something they find fascinating. See how you might be represented in their dreams.

Drawing dreams is a gratifying and interesting way to engage children in dream exploration, and it is especially helpful for the younger ones who are not yet reading and writing. Family dreamwork is a great way of telling stories together.

PLAY WITH YOUR DREAMS

It is important to realize that dreams, while sometimes significant, are not always serious. They often contain funny situations, improbable circumstances, and jokes and puns. You can use your journal to learn to play with your dreams. They are already playing with you. When you find a dream symbol or event that gives you a really good or happy feeling, bring it into your waking life. Celebrate your dreams and dream symbols: share, act out, paint, dance, smell, fantasize, wear, or eat them! Some suggestions follow.

Share them. A major reason to keep a dream journal is to be able to remember your dreams and tell them to others. Unless dreams are recorded, most of them are lost in a very short time. Use every opportunity to share what you dream with others you trust or care about. It is a gift to them and also to yourself. Many dreamers have a dreamwork partner with whom they regularly work on their week's dreams. Some people belong to groups that meet expressly for the purpose of telling and interpreting their dreams. For more information see *The Dream Sourcebook,* chapter 9.

Act them out. Using your journal as a guide, take time in a group or with friends to act out a dream or part of a dream. It may seem silly at first, but it can provide a great deal of insight. If you have others play characters in your dream, ask them what they are doing or feeling as those parts of the dream. Their responses may surprise you.

Create waking rituals. Use the symbols or images from your dreams to create rituals or sacred objects for yourself. During the day you may want to carry with you an item you dream about, or you might sleep with a certain object. Some people like to create regular practices for remembering or sharing dreams. This might involve incense or tea drinking or sitting in a quiet place in your house when recalling or working on dreams.

Program your dreams. Your dream journal can give you a chance to continue your dreams another night or to ask questions of dream characters. Program a specific activity you want more of, like flying, or give yourself a suggestion to "have a wonderful time dreaming tonight." If you have a dream or recurring dream that is unfinished, read the dream over before you go to sleep and ask your dreaming self to complete it while sleeping that evening. Repeat the dream to yourself as you are falling asleep. If you do not remember a dream in the morning, read over the journal entry you were focusing on the night before to see if it helps you remember any details to complete the dream. You can also complete the dream in waking fantasy by "finishing" the dream yourself. This is especially helpful with recurring nightmares, which often stop when they are completed in such a manner. Write down the dream story the way you would like it to turn out.

Include dreams in your creative life. Dreams expose you to your creative self and are a source of inspiration. Try writing a poem, story, or guided fantasy based on your dream (see *The Dream Sourcebook,* chapter 6). Bring images from your dream into actual parts of your life: visit a place you have dreamed about, or buy or make something that recalls a dream image. Ask yourself to dream about problems that need creative solutions. Many works of art, scientific inventions, novels, poems, and songs have been inspired by dreams (see *The Dream Sourcebook,* chapter 7). Acknowledge the value of your dreamwork by taking some of it to your workplace, perhaps posting a dream drawing on your office wall or sharing a dream insight with a coworker.

DON'T LEAVE HOME WITHOUT IT!
Take your dream journal along on trips or vacations. Many people remember their dreams more easily when traveling. New surroundings, memories, and adventures may contribute to a rich dream life on the road. Enhance your travel journals by including dream entries.

EMBRACE YOUR INNER SELF
Finally, use your journal to get to know yourself. Almost everyone who keeps a dream journal for any period of time describes it as an amazing experience. They surprise themselves with the depth and richness of their dreaming life and notice how waking events can relate to what occurs during sleep. As you review your journal you will find many such connections. You may even notice that certain dreams seem to depict events that later happen! These are called "precognitive" dreams (see *The Dream Sourcebook,* chapter 8). Though they are sometimes merely coincidence, they do happen, even with people who are not otherwise psychic. If you wish to track your potentially precognitive dreams, leave room in your journal to go back to connect dream events with happenings from your waking life.

A journal is an opportunity to see your whole self and to regularly stay in touch with your mind and spirit. Dream journals, like photographs and early school drawings, are stories about you. Keeping them is a way of valuing your history and cherishing your personal traditions. Dreams are a source of self-knowledge and discovery. We spend nearly one-third of our life asleep. Don't waste it!

THE JOURNAL

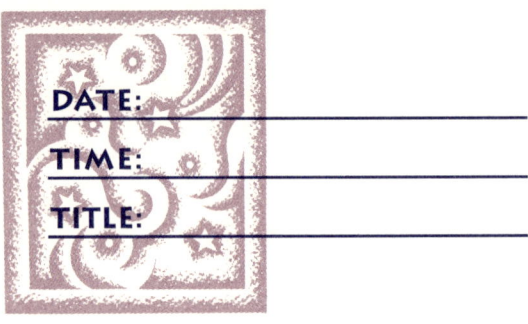

DATE:
TIME:
TITLE:

And all my days are trances,
And all my nightly dreams
Are where thy gray eye glances,
And where thy footstep gleams—
In what ethereal dances,
By what eternal streams.
   —Edgar Allan Poe, To One in Paradise

DATE:
TIME:
TITLE:

DATE:
TIME:
TITLE:

DATE: _____
TIME: _____
TITLE: _____

> There couldn't be a society of people who didn't dream.
> They'd be dead in two weeks.
>
> —William Burroughs, American author,
> with William Burroughs: *A Report from the Bunker,* "On Dreams"

DATE:
TIME:
TITLE:

DATE:
TIME:
TITLE:

What is life? A madness.
What is life? An illusion,
a shadow, a story.
And the greatest good
is little enough: for all life is
a dream, and dreams themselves
are only dreams.
  —Pedro Calderon de la Barca, *Life Is a Dream*

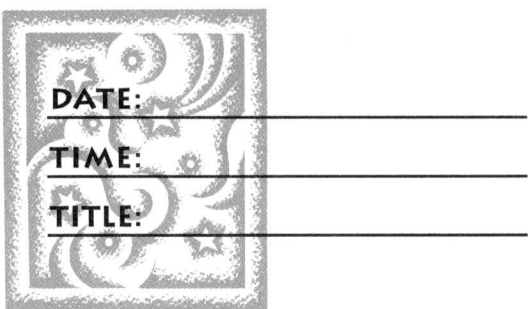

DATE: _____

TIME: _____

TITLE: _____

Really become the thing—whatever it is in a dream—become it . . . and stop thinking. Lose your mind and come to your senses.
—Frederick S. Perls, psychotherapist

DATE:
TIME:
TITLE:

DATE:
TIME:
TITLE:

If there were dreams to sell,
What would you buy?
Some cost a passing-bell;
Some a light sigh.
    —Thomas Lovell Beddoes, *Dream Pedlary*

DATE:
TIME:
TITLE:

DATE:
TIME:
TITLE:

> *I dream, therefore I exist.*
> —J. August Strindberg,
> Swedish dramatist, novelist, and poet

DATE:
TIME:
TITLE:

DATE:
TIME:
TITLE:

DATE:
TIME:
TITLE:

There are two gates of Sleep. One is of horn, easy of passage for the shades of truth; the other, of gleaming white ivory, permits false dreams to ascend to the upper air.
—Virgil, *Aeneid*

DATE:
TIME:
TITLE:

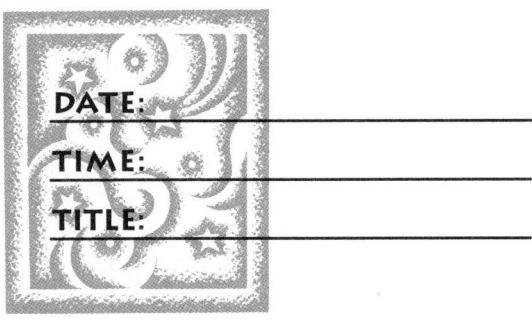

DATE: _____
TIME: _____
TITLE: _____

What can it mean? you ask. I answer not
For meaning, but myself must echo, What?
And tell it as I saw it on the spot.
  —Christina Rossetti, English poet, "My Dream"

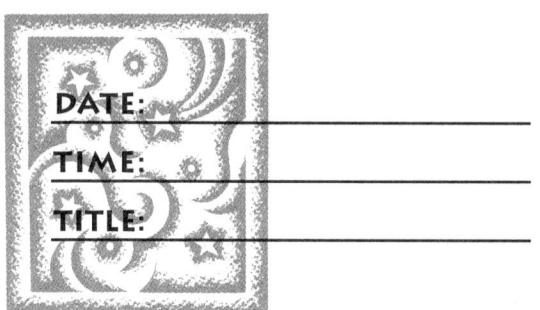

DATE:
TIME:
TITLE:

> Here, where the world is quiet;
> Here, where all trouble seems
> Dead winds' and spent waves' riot
> In doubtful dreams of dreams.
>
> —Algernon Charles Swinburne, English poet,
> "The Garden of Proserpine"

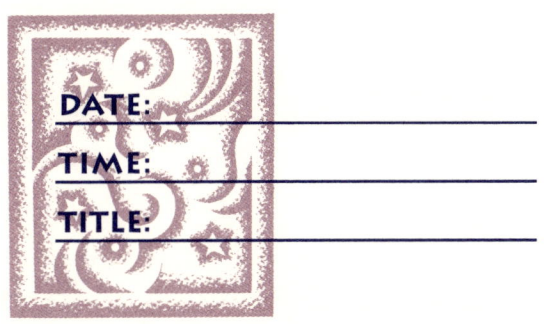

DATE: _____
TIME: _____
TITLE: _____

DATE: _____
TIME: _____
TITLE: _____

> Dreams are often most profound
> when they seem most crazy.
>
> —Sigmund Freud,
> The Interpretation of Dreams

DATE: _____
TIME: _____
TITLE: _____

DATE:
TIME:
TITLE:

DATE:
TIME:
TITLE:

> *In bed my real love has always been the sleep that rescued me by allowing me to dream.*
> —Silia in *The Rules of the Game*,
> Luigi Pirandello, Italian author and playwright

DATE:
TIME:
TITLE:

DATE:
TIME:
TITLE:

We must at least agree that the things seen by us in sleep are . . . like painted images and cannot have been formed save in the likeness of what is real and true.
    —René Descartes

DATE: _____
TIME: _____
TITLE: _____

> We are the music-makers,
> And we are the dreamers of dreams,
> Wandering by lone sea breakers,
> And sitting by desolate streams . . .
> —Arthur William Edgar O'Shaughnessy, *Ode*

DATE: _____
TIME: _____
TITLE: _____

DATE: _____

TIME: _____

TITLE: _____

But I, being poor, have only my dreams;
I have spread my dreams under your feet;
Tread softly because you tread on my dreams.
    —William Butler Yeats, Irish poet, "The Wing Among the Reeds"

DATE:
TIME:
TITLE:

DATE:
TIME:
TITLE:

DATE:
TIME:
TITLE:

One of the characteristics of the dream is that nothing surprises us in it. With no regret, we agree to live in it with strangers, completely cut off from our habits and friends.
— Jean Cocteau, French author and filmmaker

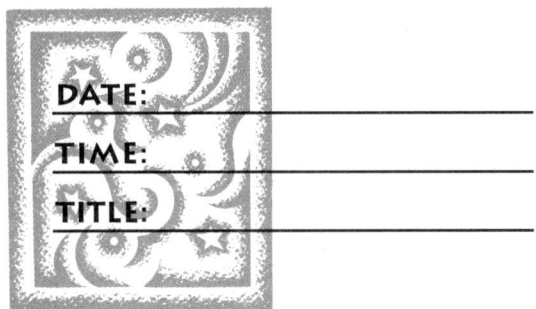

DATE:
TIME:
TITLE:

DATE: _____

TIME: _____

TITLE: _____

We wake from one dream into another dream.
—Ralph Waldo Emerson,
 "Illusions" in *The Conduct of Life*

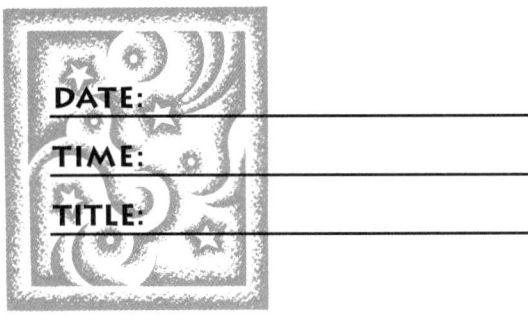

DATE: _____
TIME: _____
TITLE: _____

*It is up to you to choose your own path,
to discover your route on the map,
to lead yourself to your source
through the study of your dreams.*
   —Phyllis Koch-Sheras, Ph.D., and Amy Lemley,
   The Dream Sourcebook

DATE: _____
TIME: _____
TITLE: _____

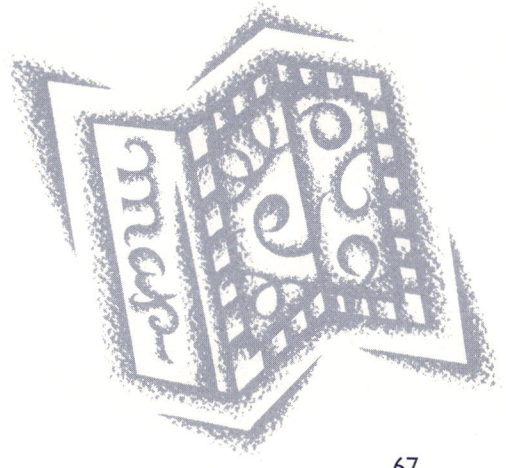

DATE: _____
TIME: _____
TITLE: _____

DATE: _____
TIME: _____
TITLE: _____

There is a prodigious selfishness in dreams: They live perfectly deaf and invulnerable amid the cries of the real world.
  —George Santayana, Spanish-born American poet and philosopher

DATE:
TIME:
TITLE:

DATE:
TIME:
TITLE:

*There are more things in heaven and earth, Horatio,
Than are dreamt of in your philosophy.*
—William Shakespeare, *Hamlet*

DATE:
TIME:
TITLE:

*That which the dream shows is
the shadow of such wisdom
as exists in man,
even if during his waking state
he may know nothing about it.*
 —Paracelsus

DATE:
TIME:
TITLE:

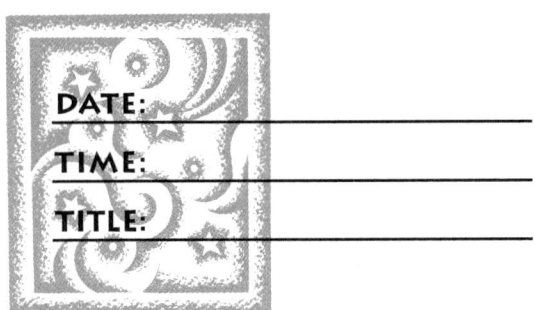

DATE: _____
TIME: _____
TITLE: _____

> The interpretation of dreams
> is the royal road to a knowledge
> of the unconscious activities of the mind.
> —Sigmund Freud,
> *The Interpretation of Dreams*

DATE: _____
TIME: _____
TITLE: _____

DATE: _____
TIME: _____
TITLE: _____

DATE: _____
TIME: _____
TITLE: _____

*I can never decide
whether my dreams are
the result of my thoughts,
or my thoughts the result
of my dreams . . . But my
dreams make conclusions
for me. They decide things
finally. I dream a decision.
Sleep seems to hammer out
for me the logical conclusions
of my vague days, and offer me
them as dreams.*
  —D. H. Lawrence, British novelist

DATE: _____
TIME: _____
TITLE: _____

DATE: _____
TIME: _____
TITLE: _____

*If a man, sitting all alone, cannot dream strange things,
and make them look like truth,
he need never try to write romances.*
 —Nathaniel Hawthorne, *The Scarlet Letter*

DATE: _____
TIME: _____
TITLE: _____

Was it a vision, or a waking dream?
Fled is that music:—Do I wake or sleep?
   —John Keats, "Ode to a Nightingale"

DATE:

TIME:

TITLE:

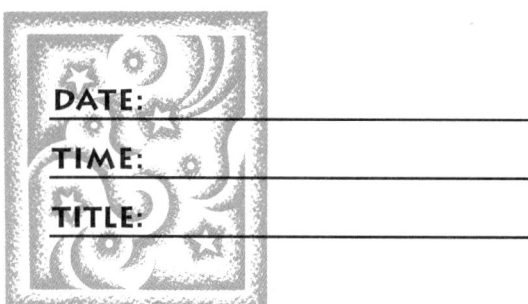

DATE: _____
TIME: _____
TITLE: _____

> To all, to each, a fair goodnight,
> And pleasing dreams, and slumbers light!
> —Sir Walter Scott, Marmion, *L'Envoy*

DATE: _____
TIME: _____
TITLE: _____

DATE:
TIME:
TITLE:

DATE:
TIME:
TITLE:

My dreams are my own doing.
I "do" me when I "dream" me.
  —John Weir, Gestalt therapist

DATE:
TIME:
TITLE:

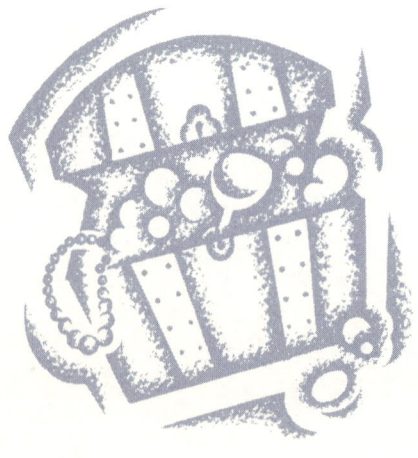

DATE:
TIME:
TITLE:

> *The treasures are there,
> hidden in the mystery
> and complexity
> of your dreamworld,
> and the discovery will
> come as long as
> you continue to search.*
>
> —Phyllis Koch-Sheras,
> E. Ann Hollier,
> and Brooke Jones,
> *Dream On:
> A Dream Interpretation and
> Exploration Guide for Women*

DATE: _____
TIME: _____
TITLE: _____

It is best to treat a dream as one would treat a totally unknown object: one looks at it from all sides, takes it in one's hand, carries it about, has all sorts of ideas and fantasies about it, and talks of it to other people.
—Carl Jung

DATE:
TIME:
TITLE:

DATE:
TIME:
TITLE:

*I dream in my dream all the dreams of the other dreamers,
And I become the other dreamers.*
   —Walt Whitman, *The Sleepers*

DATE:
TIME:
TITLE:

> *The armoured cars of dreams,*
> *contrived to let us do*
> *so many a dangerous thing.*
>
> —Elizabeth Bishop, American poet,
> "Sleeping Standing Up"

DATE: _____
TIME: _____
TITLE: _____

DATE:
TIME:
TITLE:

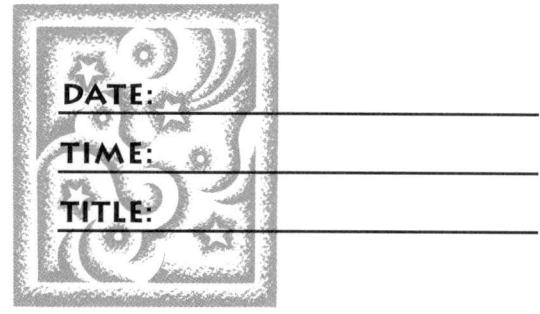

DATE:
TIME:
TITLE:

We often forget our dreams so speedily: if we cannot catch them as they are passing out at the door, we never set eyes on them again.
—William Hazlitt, "On Dreams" in *The Plain Speaker*

DATE:
TIME:
TITLE:

> *There's a long, long trail awinding*
> *Into the land of my dreams.*
> —Stoddard King, songwriter

DATE:
TIME:
TITLE:

DATE:
TIME:
TITLE:

An immense joy comes when the house of fear collapses and we realize the possibilities of our dreams.
—Alberto Taczo, South American shaman

DATE:
TIME:
TITLE:

DATE: _____
TIME: _____
TITLE: _____

Those who have compared our life to a dream were right . . .
We sleeping wake, and waking sleep.
 —Michel Eyquem de Montaigne

DATE:
TIME:
TITLE:

DATE:
TIME:
TITLE:

> *The eye of man hath not heard,*
> *the ear of man hath not seen,*
> *man's hand is not able to taste,*
> *his tongue to conceive,*
> *nor his heart to report*
> *what my dream was.*
>
> —Bottom in William Shakespeare's
> *A Midsummer Night's Dream*

DATE: _____
TIME: _____
TITLE: _____

> Till their own dreams at length deceive 'em,
> And oft repeating, they believe 'em.
> —Matthew Prior, English poet, "Alma"

DATE:
TIME:
TITLE:

If a little dreaming is dangerous, the cure for it is not to dream less but to dream more, to dream all the time.
   —Marcel Proust, French novelist,
     Remembrance of Things Past, vol. 4

DATE: _____
TIME: _____
TITLE: _____

DATE:
TIME:
TITLE:

DATE:
TIME:
TITLE:

> All life is a dream,
> and dreams themselves are only dreams.
> —Pedro Calderon de la Barca, *Life Is a Dream*

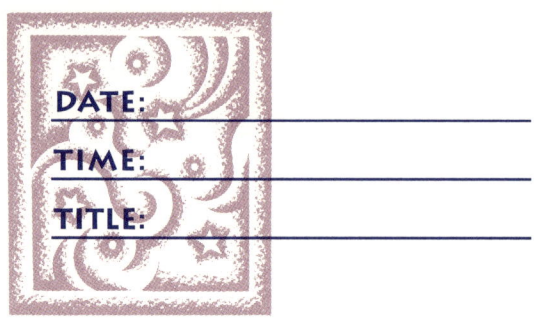

DATE:
TIME:
TITLE:

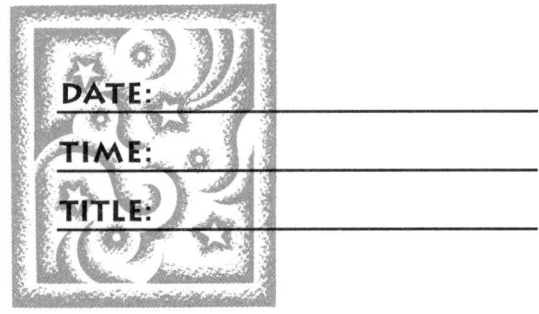

DATE:

TIME:

TITLE:

Dreaming permits each and every one of us to be quietly and safely insane every night of our lives.

—William Dement, Newsweek, 30 November 1959

DATE:
TIME:
TITLE:

> *I do not know whether*
> *I was then a man dreaming*
> *I was a butterfly,*
> *or whether I am now a butterfly*
> *dreaming I am a man.*
>
> —Chuang-tzu, *On Leveling All Things*

DATE: _____
TIME: _____
TITLE: _____

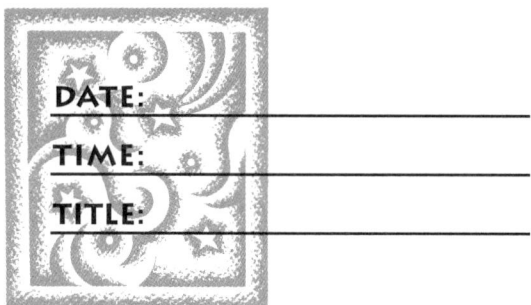

DATE: _____
TIME: _____
TITLE: _____

They who dream by day are cognizant of many things which escape those who dream only by night.
—Edgar Allan Poe, *Eleonora*

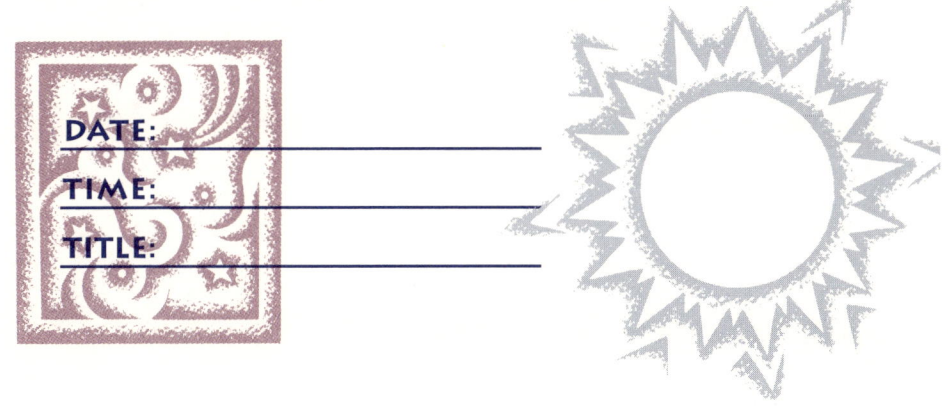

DATE:
TIME:
TITLE:

DATE:
TIME:
TITLE:

DATE: _____
TIME: _____
TITLE: _____

> *The imagination may be compared to Adam's dream—he awoke and found it truth.*
> —John Keats, English poet, in a letter to Benjamin Bailey

DATE:
TIME:
TITLE:

DATE: _____
TIME: _____
TITLE: _____

Those dreams that on the silent night intrude,
And with false flitting shades our minds delude,
Jove never sends us downward from the skies,
Nor can they from infernal mansions rise;
But all are mere productions of the brain,
And fools consult interpreters in vain.
   —Jonathan Swift, "On Dreams"

DATE:
TIME:
TITLE:

We are near awakening when we dream that we dream.
—Novalis (Baron Friedrich von Hardenberg)

DATE:
TIME:
TITLE:

DATE: _____
TIME: _____
TITLE: _____

*"Wake up, Alice dear!" said her sister. "Why, what a long sleep you've had."
"Oh, I've had such a curious dream!" said Alice.*
—Lewis Carroll, *Alice's Adventures in Wonderland*

DATE:
TIME:
TITLE:

DATE:
TIME:
TITLE:

DATE:
TIME:
TITLE:

Dreams are the touchstones of our characters.
—Henry David Thoreau

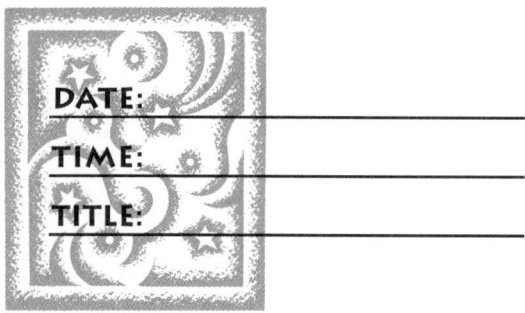

DATE: _____

TIME: _____

TITLE: _____

Those things that have occupied a man's thoughts and affections while awake recur to his imagination while asleep.
　—St. Thomas Aquinas

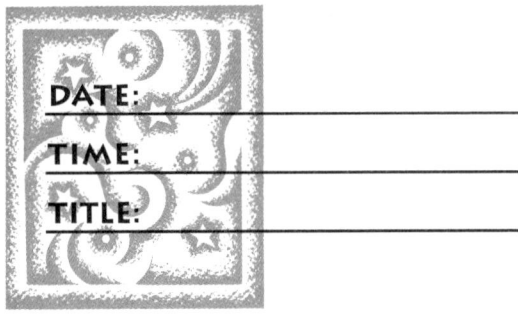

DATE: _____
TIME: _____
TITLE: _____

Many's the long night I've dreamed of cheese—toasted, mostly.
　—Robert Louis Stevenson, *Treasure Island*

DATE:
TIME:
TITLE:

DATE:
TIME:
TITLE:

Every experience on the physical, astral or mental plane is just a dream before the soul.
—Hazrat Inayat Khan

DATE:
TIME:
TITLE:

DATE:
TIME:
TITLE:

DATE:

TIME:

TITLE:

> Everything that man esteems
> Endures a moment or a day.
> Love's pleasure drives his love away,
> The painter's brush consumes his dreams.
>
> —William Butler Yeats, Irish poet, "Youth and Age"

DATE: _____
TIME: _____
TITLE: _____

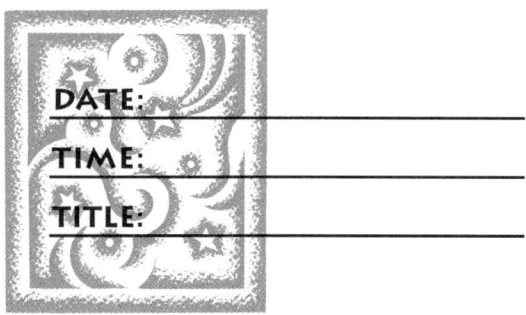

DATE: _____
TIME: _____
TITLE: _____

*Dreams are faithful interpreters of our inclinations;
but there is art required to sort and understand them.*
  —Montaigne, "Of Experience" in *Essays*

DATE:
TIME:
TITLE:

DATE:
TIME:
TITLE:

We live as we dream—alone.
   —Joseph Conrad, English novelist,
     Heart of Darkness

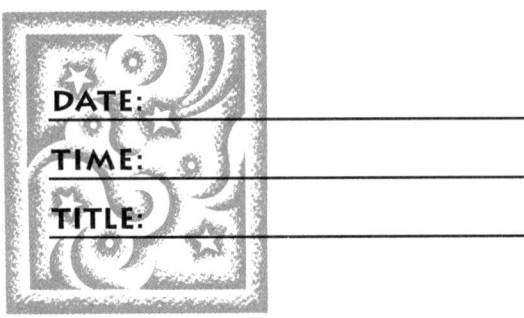

DATE: _____
TIME: _____
TITLE: _____

Tell me not, in mournful numbers,
Life is but an empty dream!
For the soul is dead that slumbers,
And things are not what they seem.
    —Henry Wadsworth Longfellow, *A Psalm of Life*

DATE:
TIME:
TITLE:

DATE:

TIME:

TITLE:

DATE:
TIME:
TITLE:

> A sweet thing, for whatever time,
> to revisit in dreams
> the dear dead we have lost.
>
> —Euripides, *Alcestis*

DATE:
TIME:
TITLE:

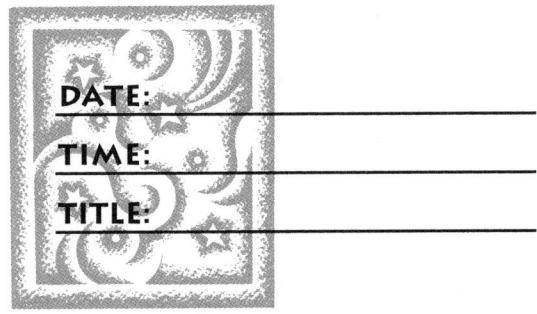

DATE:
TIME:
TITLE:

Whither is fled the visionary gleam?
Where is it now, the glory and the dream?
   —William Wordsworth, *Intimations of Immortality*

DATE:
TIME:
TITLE:

> Sleep not, dream not; this bright day
> Will not, cannot last for aye;
> Bliss like thine is bought by years
> Dark with torment and with tears.
>
> —Emily Bronte, "Sleep Not"

DATE:
TIME:
TITLE:

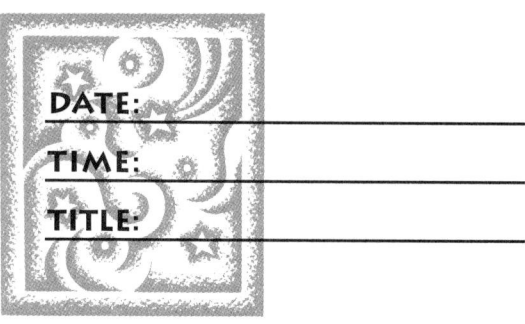

DATE: _____

TIME: _____

TITLE: _____

*[Jacob] dreamed, and behold
a ladder set up on the earth,
and the top of it reached
to heaven: and behold
the angels of God ascending
and descending on it.*
—The Bible, Genesis 28:12

DATE:
TIME:
TITLE:

DATE:
TIME:
TITLE:

DATE:
TIME:
TITLE:

Hope is a waking dream.
—Aristotle, Diogenes Laertius,
  Lives of Eminent Philosophers

DATE: _____
TIME: _____
TITLE: _____

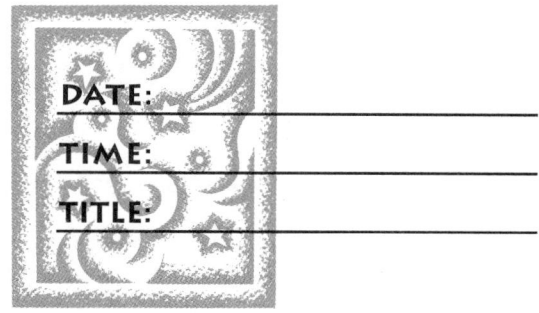

DATE:
TIME:
TITLE:

Last night I dreamed I ate a ten-pound marshmallow, and when I woke up the pillow was gone.

—Tommy Cooper, *1,191 Best Things Anybody Ever Said*

DATE:
TIME:
TITLE:

> Wavering between the profit and the loss
> In this brief transit where the dreams cross
> The dream crossed twilight between birth and dying.
> —T.S. Eliot, *Ash Wednesday*

DATE:
TIME:
TITLE:

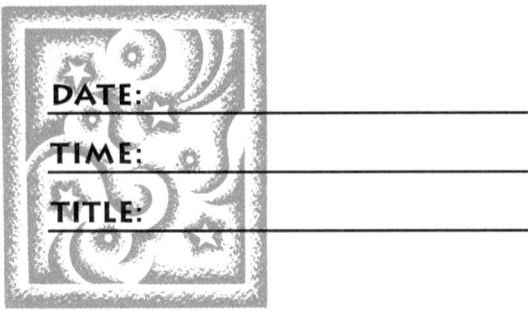

DATE:
TIME:
TITLE:

The waking have one world in common;
sleepers have each a private world of his own.
—Heraclitus, *Fragments*

DATE:
TIME:
TITLE:

DATE:
TIME:
TITLE:

DATE:
TIME:
TITLE:

A sight to dream of, not to tell!
—Samuel Taylor Coleridge, *The Rime of the Ancient Mariner*

DATE:
TIME:
TITLE:

DATE:

TIME:

TITLE:

*Deep into that darkness peering, long I stood there wondering, fearing,
Doubting, dreaming dreams no mortal ever dared to dream before.*
—Edgar Allan Poe, *The Raven*

DATE:
TIME:
TITLE:

DATE: _____
TIME: _____
TITLE: _____

I slept and dreamed that life was beauty,
I woke—and found that life was duty.
    —Ellen Sturgis Hooper, *Beauty and Duty*

DATE:

TIME:

TITLE:

Try to wash your mind before you go to sleep like you brush your teeth; then your dreams will be clear.
—Tenzin W. Rinpoche, Tibetan teacher

DATE: _____
TIME: _____
TITLE: _____

DATE:
TIME:
TITLE:

Vain hopes are often like the dreams of those who wake.
—Quintilian, De Institutione Oratoria

DATE: _____
TIME: _____
TITLE: _____

DATE:
TIME:
TITLE:

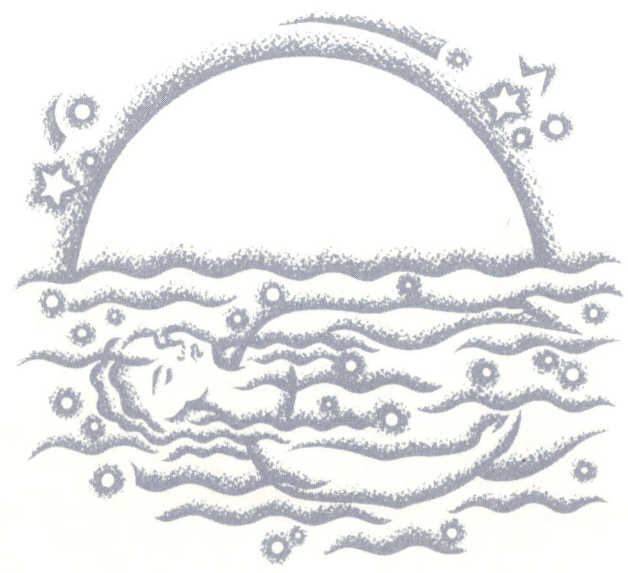

DATE: _____
TIME: _____
TITLE: _____

> To sleep: Perchance to dream: ay, there's the rub:
> For in that sleep of death what dreams may come
> When we have shuffled off this mortal coil,
> Must give us pause.
>
> —Hamlet in William Shakespeare's *Hamlet*

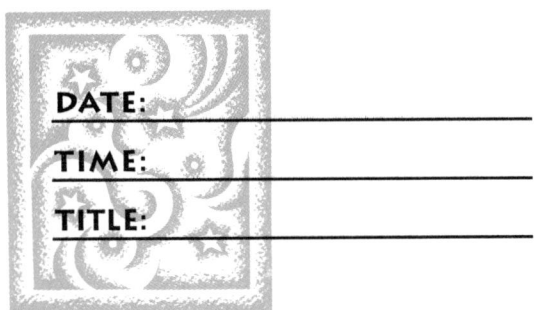

DATE: _____
TIME: _____
TITLE: _____

> *Dreamer of dreams, born out of my due time,*
> *why should I stive to set the crooked straight?*
> —William Morris, The Earthly Paradise, An Apology

DATE:
TIME:
TITLE:

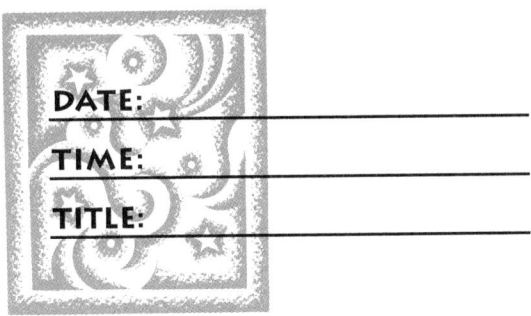

DATE:
TIME:
TITLE:

About ten days ago, I retired very late . . . I soon began to dream.
There seemed to be death-like stillness about me . . .
There was a throng of people, some gazing mournfully upon the corpse, whose face was covered, others weeping pitifully.
"Who is dead in the White House?" I demanded of one of the soldiers.
"The President," was his answer, "he was killed by an assassin!"
 —Ward Hill Lamon, *Recollections of Abraham Lincoln*

DATE: _____
TIME: _____
TITLE: _____

DATE:
TIME:
TITLE:

DATE:
TIME:
TITLE:

*Give us long rest or death,
dark death or dreamful ease.*
—Lord Alfred Tennyson, *The Lotus Eaters*

DATE:
TIME:
TITLE:

DATE: _____
TIME: _____
TITLE: _____

Dreams and beasts are two keys by which we find out the secrets of our own nature.
—Ralph Waldo Emerson

YOUR PERSONAL DREAM INDEX

ABOUT THE PERSONAL DREAM INDEX

This Index provides a wonderful resource with which to explore your dreams. After circling key dream elements (objects, characters, symbols, and themes); underlining emotion-stirring phrases or segments; and perhaps noting incidences of lucidity, dreaming in color, or anything else that seems remarkable to you, turn to the Personal Dream Index. Organize your dream data by entering the key elements alphabetically, noting the page on which each entry appears. As certain key dream elements recur—and they will—you will have a clear record for use in dreamwork. Simply turn to the pages you've noted.

Here is an example of the Dream Index in action. The dreamer has a dream about a map. Upon waking, the dreamer writes the dream in this journal, using the first person, present tense: "I am lost along a country road. I find a map in a ditch." The dreamer then circles key elements and underlines strong emotional phrases or passages. In this dream, one of the key dream elements is a map. When the dream has been recorded, the dreamer turns to the Index and follows this simple procedure:

1. Enter the key word (map) under the appropriate letter (M). If an entry for that word exists already, go to the next step.
2. Write the page number on which the current dream appears (84).
3. Using the Index, go back to the journal and review the other dreams that contain the same symbol (map). In this example, dreams on pages 42, 67, and 70 also include a map as a key element. What does that mean? Only the dreamer knows for sure.

The sample entry looks like this:

Megan (daughter), 38, 79,

Medicine, 27

Monster, 63

Map 42, 67, 70, 84

Naked flying, 52, 98

Needle, 57

Net, 134

Nun, 44, 56, 65, 79, 82, 97, 123

Newt Gingrich, 68

O P

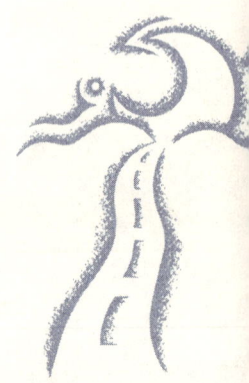